SURPRISE ME, JESUS

SURPRISE ME, JESUS

Herbert F. Brokering

AUGSBURG PUBLISHING HOUSE
Minneapolis, Minnesota

SURPRISE ME, JESUS

Copyright © 1973 Augsburg Publishing House

Library of Congress Catalog Card No. 73-83785

International Standard Book No. 0-8066-1338-6

Manufactured in the United States of America

Jesus surprises.
He comes, where there's nothing going on,
where it's too soon, when it's not time,
when no one is looking,
when someone can't wait any longer,
where there's no one around.
Surprise me, Jesus, is a statement of belief
that he already has
and that he will surprise.
Surprise Me, Jesus contains 80 prayers
good for someone alone,
with another,
in a family, a community, a large gathering,
and it is good
as a gift to someone,
and to yourself.

Herb Brokering

Contents

When Only a Song Can Say It

Lord, I can't live
where there isn't feeling.
It's better for me to have anger
than to not feel anything at all.
Thinking is not enough.
Thoughts are not everything.
I also have my feelings,
which are so much of me.
Lord, I feel more holy,
when I feel more rhythm.
The more I dance and sing,
the holier life seems to be.
Give me ways
to do my feelings, Jesus.

Give Me Ways to Do My Feelings

Lord, thank you for all the colors.
It's beautiful that
music sounds can come in color,
that bars and measures of songs
can be more than print,
and that sound is more than notes.
Some songs I like
look like rainbows swirling in technicolor.
Some songs are like black and white,
or red and yellow,
sometimes standing still, sometimes swirling.
I can wonder about the color of the trumpet sound,
what is the brightest colored hymn,
and why some songs have no color.
Keep connecting colors and sounds
in my imagination, Jesus.

Connect Color and Sounds

Lord, who are those who play the instruments
and what is behind their tunes?
Is there a sigh and weeping
in the woodwinds?
Is there a lover calling in the piccolo?
Is there an angry man shouting
in the French horn,
and a jilted girl crying
in the oboe?
Is there a coward screaming
in the snare drum?
Help me hear the feelings of people
in the piccolo
in the French horn, the oboe,
and in the snare drum.
Give to those who play
laughter and love in their rhythm.
Redeem us people, Lord
in the strings of guitars.
Save us people,
in the tight skins of drums, Jesus.

Help Me Hear the Feelings of People

Lord, turn me on to the Bible.
Give it to me in a new way.
What if the Bible could be set to rhythm
and every holy story were a song?
Lord, it would be even more fantastic.
And what if I could feel
some of your stories in songs,
with their strong beat,
and their deep meanings?
I like to think
of holy things.
Lord, turn me on to your Word,
and to the Bible's beat,
and the refrain.
Lord, let me hear it.
So let me hear the story like new,
and be turned on, Jesus.

The Bible's Beat

Lord, I had a song on the tip of my tongue;
I could not sing it.
It was on the tip of my finger;
I could not touch it.
It was on the top of my head;
I could not remember it.
It was at the bottom of my heart;
I could not find it.
Then I heard a song somewhere,
for the first time.
It is my song,
though I have never composed.
Someone brought it
out of the bottom of my heart.
If I could write,
I would have written it.
If I could sing it,
I would, Jesus.

It Is My Song

Lord, I thank you for drummers—
that I can think
of everything I know
as played on a drum—
not with a magic marker, or pencil, or in writing,
but with a stick on a drum.
It seems to me, Lord,
that all words are in the drum.
With the drums
I could speak any language
and say anything.
If I could take a foreign language, Lord,
I'd take drums
and travel around the world with them.
I could go anywhere with drums
and repeat the story of creation.
Then it would have its beat.
Keep holding all created things together, Jesus.

I'd Take Drums

Lord, the towns and air waves
are full of popular songs.
Come to me
when only a song can say it,
and when I get marooned.
Come to me
when only a recording can tell me.
Come when the lyrics are a true story
and I am in the story.
And the longer it plays
and the louder it may be,
the more quiet it gets to be in me.
If I'm easy to find
in some new song,
sing it to me, and find me in the song.
Sing it to me, Jesus.
Sing it to me, Jesus.

When Only a Song Can Say It

What Do I Do with All the Rules?

Lord, the politicians are at it.
They are discussing matters of life and death.
They are voting what to do with the poor and the rich,
what to do with leftover food and untapped wells.
They are deciding what belongs to which people.
They are writing bylaws about the hungry, the needy,
and about the truth.
World and God, man and God—is what it's all about, Jesus.
The politicians are hired to do what you talked about—
to live for the poor, the rich,
the lonely, the earth, and the truth.
There seems to be so much these days
for politicians to sit and decide about.
Lord, seat them at your right hand.
Give them the eyes to see the will of the Father
as their work.
We need your spirit in all the laws, Jesus.

Your Spirit in Our Laws

Lord, I can drive.
Speed and power and love
are at my fingertips.
I can steer horsepower with one or two hands.
I can break and obey road laws with my foot.
Now there are new ways to be a friend or enemy
at speed zones and intersections and on curves.
There are new ways to get even.
I know what it's like
to behave with hundreds of horsepower,
what it's like to be first or last,
and what it's like to have someone crowd me out
an inch from death.
I know injustice on the road.
I have a new feeling about laws since I drive.
Lord,
my insides and heart show on the road.
Test my love in your way,
when I drive, Jesus.

I Can Steer Horsepower

Lord, I feel like a war veteran
in my youth.
I feel like eighty,
and my hair feels white.
I am like shell shocked.
I've been through wars.
I have thousands of enemies
filing past me,
who never see me, while I hide.
I could destroy them,
but I have no weapon.
I'm starving,
and I need someone to eat with me.
I feel like a veteran of battles, Lord,
and I'm afraid of being cut off by my enemies.
I am hiding behind this large rock, Jesus.

I've Been Through Wars

Lord, what do I do with all the rules?
I do not know where many began, or what they mean.
I do not know if they are true for me.
Some I do not like.
Some are written, and some are in the air.
Some have no names.
Some are on signs and in songs.
Some are inside of me. Some are invisible.
Lord, what I need is to feel the inside of the rules.
I need to see the spirit of them—
the heart of them.
I want to know how rules feel to people.
I want the life and the beat of the law, Jesus.

The Inside of the Rules

Lord, what is the meaning of a grade?
What does it mean to be average, or above it?
Is it right to think of myself as below average?
What does grading do to me?
Make me think it through.
Will the grades separate me from others?
Do they tell me something that isn't true about myself?
What do I do with grades?
What do you do with them, Lord?
Do I use them to get what I want
or to excuse myself?
What besides grades tells me who I am?
I know that to you I am an A, Jesus.
You know what it means to be treated like a failure,
though you were perfect.
You give me courage, Jesus.

The Meaning of a Grade

Lord, I wonder at all the books there are.
I wonder how high they'd be stacked,
or how much land they'd cover if spread out.
What a thing books can be.
In a tiny book I can go into another generation.
In a novel I can join people in their real life.
In a short story I can go into a war-torn land.
In a paperback I can travel on trips I could never afford.
So I'm glad for the books.
In them keep me in touch with your world,
and with myself,
and with these times.
Lord, keep my imagination open
to travel in all sorts of worlds
through human writing and reading.
We thank you that you have also humbled yourself
to the printing press.
You are truly the Word in the flesh, Jesus.

I'm Glad for the Books

Lord, why do we like clothes so much?
Why do clothes take up so much of my space and time?
I know those clothes which are on my mind.
I know when clothes are missing,
and when someone else's clothes are mixed with mine.
I can hide in them,
and I can communicate through them.
They are more than covering.
So Lord, I'll talk about my clothes
as your gift to me.
Remember the naked and the needy, Jesus.

About My Clothes

Lord, I have habits.
They are sure ways which I know myself.
I do them over and over,
as though my life depends on them.
Some habits are against my life;
some habits keep me alive;
and some habits will destroy me.
Lord, I need to deal with the habits
which are deep inside me.
My habits are myself,
and so I know you care about them.
Look at my habits, Jesus.

Look at My Habits

Lord, it is urgent
that I give away my new ideas.
I cannot keep them all to myself.
To whom do I tell them?
Some of them I will throw out
like seed into the wind.
But there are those which I must tell
in a careful way.
My thoughts are myself.
Yet I have them from someone else;
and now I must tell them.
Give me the spirit to tell my thoughts.
Send me those who will add mine to theirs,
so we can raise up newer ideas.
Make your spirit blow
like wind to keep good thoughts flying, Jesus.

My New Ideas

Lord, there are so many things
I do without thinking.
They are the automatic things,
that must be done
when there isn't time to think.
They are the habits,
the involuntary acts of my life.
I have no control over some habits.
They were placed into me in birth,
and they are part of the age-long system
that keeps me alive.
Some are actions I have learned
through the years of my life.
I am thankful for the many things
that go in and around me
about which I need not think, or worry.
They are really your gift.
I think about them now to thank you.
And as I go on living,
I thank you for them
even when I do not think about them, Jesus.

When There Isn't Time to Think

Lord, I do not hate the millions
at whom our missiles point.
They are not my enemy.
I did not declare a war on them.
When the destruction is over,
when the dust settles,
and the war is settled,
I will rise to bring peace.
I will volunteer;
I will plant trees in the torn land
and water them
in the name of the Father,
and the Son, and the Holy Spirit.
I do not understand wars,
nor can I fathom the forgiveness
of the millions who suffer.
I do not know them
or hate them, Jesus.

I Do Not Hate the Millions

Lord, I have been very busy,
and I am caught up in the schedule.
Your gift of time
has grabbed hold of me like a prison.
I am being crucified
each day and night
on some calendar of events,
and I cry out to you each day
from my 30-day paper cross.
Give me back my 30 days per month,
and my weeks and hours.
I want to live in your spirit in freedom.
Make me a good steward of time.
Make me love time
and take it as your gift to me
hour by hour, Jesus.

Your Gift of Time

Lord, I'm not in the war.
I dislike my neighbors,
I can't stand teachers,
and I despise my own relatives,
but I'm not in the war.
I dread someone's voice,
can't stand someone's breath,
and someone's complaining drives me crazy,
but I'm not in the war.
I never talk to some people,
and it wouldn't help anything if I did,
because you know how it is,
but I'm not in the war.
I need peace in all this war, Jesus.

I Need Peace

Lord, give us a national anthem.
We need something musical
for courage and loyalty.
We need something to make us more human,
to tie us together,
and to free us.
Give us songs we can know by heart
and sing out loud
when we need them.
Lord, if we could play more songs,
if we sang more music,
then we'd run out of wars.
Give us more national anthems
for the land, Jesus.

More National Anthems

Lord, what's the heartbeat of anger
and breath that hates?
What's the rhythm of people who hate?
How do pulses go that are afraid,
and how do their minds spin?
You know, Lord.
What song can unfreeze us?
What can make us brave
and take away our fear?
Who will penetrate
our lonesomeness
and give us back our heart?
What is the rhythm
of us when we are angry,
and what songs
can we still hear?
If we in our anger
grow deaf to hymns and prayers,
send us a new song to save us.
Save us in something new,
or something old,
but save us in our anger, Jesus.

Save Us in Our Anger

Someone is Crying

Lord, I am sad.
I have opened myself to someone else's hurt.
Their pain has cut into me.
Their tears are filling up the inside of me.
Show me that through tears
I can see birds
I never saw fly or heard sing before.
Take me through the pain
to have good thoughts I did not know before.
What was buried is rising, Lord.
My broken heart is breaking up hard places.
Do not take all the tears away,
or my sight will be short
and my heart will get hard.
Soften my spirit
even if it is with tears, Jesus.

Someone Else's Hurt

Lord, help me to face death
as though I'd already been there.
I know life is terminal;
it ends.
Or is it only illness that ends?
Some people know or have guessed
that they are dying.
While my years increase, increase my life.
Put more into it.
Increase the value of the hours and minutes.
Show me more about reality.
With the future coming closer,
make today seem larger and go farther.
I want to get more out of an hour,
and bring more to this day.
Jesus, I want your way.
I want to feel sure, in the face of the unknown.
I want to live big
in the middle of not seeing for sure, Jesus.

I Know Life Is Terminal

Lord, I have the possibility to suffer.
I could get more involved.
I could get into trouble for a good cause.
There's plenty going on
and plenty of places to get into
and do something critical.
Some of it is really big, Lord.
And it could mean lots of sacrifice.
Some of it is small, and close, and personal.
I could really get involved
if I took the time,
and had the nerve, and wanted to.
That's what I need to know—
how far to go,
where to draw the line,
what to stand for.
I need to think things through
and talk things over.
What a day to be alive.
Make me alive, Jesus.
What a time to live.
Give me the mind to live, Jesus.

I Could Get Involved

Lord, I don't want to be fooled by my own fears.
I don't want to be fooled by what is not true
and never was true.
I don't want to be tricked by a scared imagination.
Put on my mind
what is true today,
even if I have not known it or faced it.
Make me face reality and learn the truth.
Take away the crippling fear
which makes me less than I am.
Lord, mean more to me.
Lord, I want to mean more to others
and to myself.
Keep telling me not to be afraid.
Be with me, Jesus.

A Scared Imagination

Lord, I am with the sick,
who wait and watch for mornings to come.
And then, we wait for the nights
and for the noons.
We wait for hours to pass.
We wait from day to day
like brittle stems in wind,
like snowflakes in warming sun,
like children on thin ice,
and people on tightropes.
Lord, give us the daring spirit
of flakes and stems,
and of skaters and walkers on high wires.
Give us the imagination
to join the life,
to live on the edges,
glad and unafraid.
May we live to your glory,
while waiting, and risking, Jesus.

Give Us a Daring Spirit

Lord, I am at a precipice.
Looking down and looking out
frightens me.
Not all can stand at this place
and take this look.
Some have fled and some have fallen.
I am in front of
the mysteries of this life.
Take from me the fear of the unknown
and the fear of the distant.
Give me a good feeling
for what is real and tangible.
Give me a heart for what's happening.
Take away the length of what's endless
and the depth of what's deep.
Give me a long look at this very minute.
Give me a clear glimpse of eternity
as you saw everlasting life
on that hill, Jesus.

Fear of the Unknown

Lord, how does one go on?
The future is part of me,
and I am going into it.
Soon it will be tomorrow.
Yesterday is barely over.
Tomorrow is barely away.
I live between;
and that's where I am now,
asking how do I go on.
It's not that I do not want it;
I ask because I am really glad
for what it means to live.
Give me a good feeling toward the present,
for I'm always coming and always going.
I am on the move, Lord;
what a surprising thing a day can be.
Keep me on the move, Jesus.

How Do I Go On?

Lord, while I am praying now,
someone is losing life.
While I am here alive
and making plans for the future,
someone is dying.
While I have it good,
someone is in trouble.
While I celebrate,
someone is in sorrow.
While I am glad,
someone is crying.
Lord, this world needs life.
I need to see ahead,
to be sure,
to be unafraid,
to know for sure where the life is.
You have assured me of life.
And so I celebrate in this dying world,
for I am sure, I expect, and I see.
Keep me celebrating
until the end,
and then give me a celebration
that no eye has ever seen, except you, Jesus.

Someone Is Crying

Lord, I do not like the end of things.
I do not like leaving,
quitting, dying, ending.
I like living.
I like as much of it as I can have.
I like life in others, in nature,
in a party, in a meeting,
in a classroom, wherever.
I like life better than death.
You did not like death.
You asked that it not happen
if possible.
You lived as though death was not the end.
You lived as though life
were stronger than a grave.
That is what I need to know.
That is how I need to face the future:
as though life is stronger
and keeps on going, Jesus.

Life Better Than Death

Your World Is Good

Lord, nature is your gift to me.
Help me to use it in faith.
If I stand under the sky,
I can ask you deep questions.
If I look to the stars,
I can ask you why.
If I look at the Milky Way,
I can be amazed.
I do not yet know how great your world is.
But it has helped me
to ask deep questions,
and to wonder,
and to ask you why, Jesus.

I Can Ask You Why

Lord, give me respect for the sun.
I cannot think
what would it be like if there were no light.
I like the sun
and all the light that goes with day and night.
What if children had no sparklers?
What if there were no strobe lights and no spotlights?
What if all colored lights went out,
and there were no Christmas lights?
What if there were no candles?
Lord, I like lights.
So I'm thankful for all the people
who sketch and design and make lights
and those who pour candles.
I am thankful for your miracle of the sun, Jesus.

I Like the Sun

Lord, I marvel at weather changes.
A season goes and a new one comes to take its place.
It's like a relay race
that is never finished.
Life never quits getting new.
The future keeps coming, and the past keeps leaving.
Every day is a new frontier.
The time for being a pioneer is not done.
Life goes on.
Life is powerful and there is so much of it.
It blows from trees, to the earth,
and digs itself out of the ground.
Life comes and comes in the watery seasons
deep in the depth of the oceans.
Life is so ever-present, an ever-living thing.
Lord, you are the creator of all of it.
Thanks for a world without end, Jesus.

Life Comes and Comes

Lord, make me conscious of my life.
I feel my pulse.
My heart beats. My life is.
I can feel it the way my mother
felt it in her, and she was glad.
I am glad too
for my life,
when I feel my heart beat
in excitement, after running,
and after good news.
My heart has a way
of taking care of things
that matter a lot.
It takes care daily, silently,
over what is beyond my control.
I need not think about it often to be grateful;
nor do I want to take my life for granted.
May the continual beat of my heart
be a sign, Lord,
of your everlasting life.
May this life of mine
celebrate the life yet to come, Jesus.

My Heart Has a Way

Lord, it is time to celebrate.
There is life,
and there are the signs of life
above, around, below, and inside.
There is life in the movements
of the leaves and the branches,
in the movements
of the birds in flight, finding food, and resting.
There are the movements
of the beast and every running and crawling thing.
There is life in the motion
of muscles on the move,
of minds on the move,
of masses on the move.
It is alive here.
Lord of life,
I celebrate all this life
with my own life.
I wish a happy birthday to the world, Jesus.

All This Life

Lord, thank you for the cycles.
You gave us the seasons,
the sunsets,
and the sunrises every day.
You gave us the seasons of seed,
and the 12 full moons every year.
We can set our watches
by the tidal waves.
I can find my way
by the North Star.
Your world is no accident,
moving as though rehearsed.
I need your idea of cycles,
and moods, and rhythms, Jesus.

Your Idea of Cycles

Lord,
this is another day
like so many,
and I don't want it to be boring.
I want to remember this day.
Open my eyes to see
something happen I can remember.
Open my ears to hear
something that I can remember.
You made life to be more than a list of events.
It is a life of events,
and they happen every day.
Each day can be memorable to me.
Make this one so great a happening
that it becomes a holiday.
I need this day;
I want you to be in it, Jesus.

Be in This Day

Lord, I love to eat and drink.
I have favorite foods.
Sometimes I indulge.
Sometimes I forget I am the vine keeper,
and a caretaker of food and drink.
Lord, give me a good appetite.
Let me taste that your world is good.
Increase my respect for meals
while I drink in a world
where so many are hungry.
Increase my thanks in a world so thirsty.
I can understand
why you chose eating and drinking
in which to come to us, Jesus.

Your World Is Good

Lord, let me see the meaning of things
so I can get involved.
Let me see the meaning of the food
and join those who produce.
Let me know the meaning of medicine
and join the experimenters.
Let me know the meaning of politics
and join the lawmakers.
Let me know the meaning of housing
and join the planners.
Let me know the meaning of theater
and join the actors.
Lord,
let me get involved,
by looking for the meaning
under the work of people.
Help me ask
why—
why people invent,
act, produce food, and plan.
If I know the meaning
of what I do,
I can do it with gladness, Jesus.

Help Me Ask Why

Love Me As I Am

Lord, here I am.
I'm the one person I know best.
There's no one in the world like me.
Without me the world would not be the same.
I make a difference.
I have power.
I have ideas no one else has.
I can change what a group does by what I decide to do.
I can do more than some would think.
I want to.
With you, I can do more than I can even imagine.
So, Lord, I need to think
that I make a difference.
You made such a difference, Jesus,
and so do I, Jesus.

Lord, Here I Am

Lord, ask me questions.
Come to me in a way so I have to answer.
Ask me, Lord.
Ask me if I enjoy eating.
What is my favorite food and why?
Why do I like trees?
Am I poor?
Do I know anyone starving?
Do I care?
How much do I have?
Where am I going?
What am I able to do?
Who needs me most?
What is the smell of bread?
How do I feel about today?
Would I rather talk to someone by phone or in person?
Lord, ask me.
Ask me if I care, Lord.
I need your questions.
Ask me, Jesus.

Ask Me, Jesus

Lord, I need a mask.
I need a covering,
something that hides me a little.
Something that brings out the inside of myself.
Something I can talk through and act through.
Something I can see through.
I need a mask,
so I can sing and cry and laugh.
I need a mask
so I can be on a stage;
so I can stand in front of others
and be myself.
I need a mask
to think of all the things I am
and put them together.
I need a mask.
I need a private place, Jesus.

I Need a Mask

Lord, where am I?
Where is it happening?
What should I be doing?
Keep me open to your call each day.
Give me eyes to see and ears to hear where I am.
Forgive me as I decide.
Give me the right to be wrong.
Love me as I am.
Forgive me so I can keep the faith.
Lord, I need to take stands,
so keep forgiving me
for I keep sinning.
Give me courage
to live in your forgiveness, Jesus.

Love Me as I Am

Lord, how do I deal with evil?
How do I find my way through all the suffering in the world
and not give up?
What do I do in all the wickedness?
What do I do in those tempting times,
when it's hard to be in
and hard to stay out?
Be with me in those times.
I will deal with evil while living in it.
I know there is evil, Lord, and I know there is good.
Both are here,
and I am deciding about them, Jesus.

I Know There Is Evil

Lord, what do I do with winning?
And what is the good of losing?
I know a lot about
winning and losing.
I think a lot about it,
and I'm always in some won-or-lost column.
Give me a loss I can stand.
Give me a victory of some kind when I am losing.
Give me something I can not get without losing.
And when I lose, remind me
how Gethsemane looked like a total catastrophe,
but it was not.
Your grave looked like a total loss;
but it was in that terrible defeat
that you won, Jesus.

When I Am Losing

Lord, help me to face what is the matter.
Not facing facts doesn't seem to be the answer.
Turning away is not the way.
It doesn't last,
and I will only have to face it later.
If facing life is the problem,
then let me do that.
I will go through it and not around it.
If I cannot face it all at once,
then give it to me in pieces and sizes I can live.
Give me the nerve to ask someone to help me lift
what I cannot hold alone.
Make me face what I can face, Jesus.
Turn my face to the truth, Jesus.

I Cannot Face It All

Lord, life is true or false.
What's true?
Lord, hearing the truth is not enough.
I have heard so many answers,
and I have said them.
I have seen the truth in print.
Lord, I need more
than print and paragraphs and speeches.
I need to feel the truth,
and to know it.
Your truth is everywhere, all around,
taking place and waiting to happen.
Your truth is in the life of all of us
and in your creation.
Lead me into the truth,
to do it and have it done to me.
Then I will remember all the true words.
Lord, I don't want to get hung up
in the truth on paper;
get me into the truth in life.
Then I can remember it, Jesus.

I Have Heard So Many Answers

Lord, sometimes I need to get away.
If for a while I could just be a stranger,
unknown, anonymous.
Then after a while, at the right time,
I would come back and belong again.
I need to leave,
if only in my spirit,
and return to reclaim what I do not have.
I need to take what I am throwing away.
Send me away, Lord,
in my imagination,
and then bring me back like new.
When it is better that I leave,
make me go,
so I can come back with a glad spirit, Jesus.

Bring Me Back Like New

Lord, all these words, words, words.
Sometimes I get sick of words,
yet I need them to live.
Words wage war against me,
and yet they are the only things we have
to make peace.
Words are for making love.
Words are for lying,
and for hiding.
And they are for facing the truth.
Lord, your words never stand alone.
Words come together
like nouns and verbs,
people and places, love and forgiveness,
action and emotion, now and forever.
Words, words, words;
what a world full of words.
And still so many things that stay unsaid, Jesus.

Words, Words, Words

Lord, I am a runaway.
So often I feel that I'm packed and leaving.
Where am I?
Here I am,
feeling away, alone, lost,
in the middle of where I live.
I'm a runaway right where I am.
This place is not always my home.
In some quick action,
or by some right person,
help me to unpack, to belong,
and to name this place our place.
Jesus, make me be at home,
here, Jesus.

Help Me Unpack

Lord, the past is part of me.
I need the times and places past,
to live where I am.
I need past times to go on.
My past is stored inside me.
It gives me the eyes I have for this day.
Help me not to deny my past,
but to face it.
Help me to take it with forgiveness,
and with celebration,
for my new thoughts come from the old thoughts.
Let the hurts of yesterday
not get me down;
let the honors not fool me.
But let me take both of them,
for they are clay in my hand.
I can throw them to the ground,
or juggle them in the air.
But I must do something with my past.
I cannot just stand here,
or say I never was.
I was, Jesus, I was,
and that makes me who I am, Jesus.

My Past Is Stored

Lord, I worry about some of my words.
They are empty and hollow.
Their meaning is gone.
I profane them.
I can make a good word into nothing.
I use it to fill space; it's a cheap way to talk,
and I can use it to cover my real feelings.
Lord, give me a respect for my vocabulary.
Increase my words.
Bless the words I know.
Bless my old words and fill up those that are empty.
Put more meaning into them.
Make them be true and good.
Lord, what would we be without our words?
Speech is your free gift to me.
Fill my words with memories.
Hear me. Hear me in my words, Jesus.
It's where I am, Jesus.

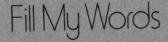

Fill My Words

We Have One Another

Lord, I need to rediscover in myself someone childlike.
It is not something I can do alone.
The child in me is lost
as a child can be lost,
and I need someone with a playful spirit
to help me hunt.
Send someone to me
who enjoys candle light,
sunlight or moonlight,
and who loves the magic, marvelling spirit in me.
Call out the child in me
to be with others
of a childlike spirit.
I want to live today
with my eyes wide open and startled
and pressed against your world with wonder.
Amaze me, Jesus.

Send Someone to Me

Lord, where have all my neighbors gone?
Where are all those who meant so much for so long?
Who are all these people moving in and moving out,
and past each other;
and why do we miss each other so much?
There's such a swift shuffle of persons faceless and nameless,
of all ages.
What a family all these could make for me,
and what a list of relatives they would be.
Lord, enlarge my relationships,
and get me out of this tiny way
of seeing people, and missing them, Jesus.

Why Do We Miss Each Other?

Lord, there is this blaming going on.
Taking blame and putting it onto others.
Being blamed for nothing you did and being made small.
Being compared to someone you're not
and never could be.
Being treated like a carbon copy of someone else.
Being forced into a pattern that isn't your shape.
And, Lord, I'm learning to blame,
and I'm doing it to others.
How can we stop tearing each other down?
How can we build each other up?
How can we keep from being puppets?
How can we enjoy our differences?
Lord, how can we need each other?
Remind me of what I do well.
Drive the blaming out of my mind, Jesus.

Drive This Blaming Out

Lord, where are the gaps in need of the bridges?
Where are the deep crevices in need of long staffs
and sure-footed shepherds who don't stumble?
Where are the ditches that need closing,
and the gullies that need home-made dams of children?
Who are those who cut into bits and pieces what is whole,
and tear apart what is one piece?
Lord, if I am the bridge, make me a strong bridge.
Send me the traffic.
If I am the dam, send me the floods.
If I am the shepherd staff,
send me someone lost who needs me.
If I am in the gap, send me some bridge.
When I am fallen, find me, Jesus.

Send Me Some Bridge

Lord, people aren't all the same.
Some help, and I don't know it.
Some need more help than they can give.
Some see me and some look past me.
Some who are near me
are irresponsible toward me.
They don't know what to say,
and they have little to ask.
Lord, I need people to get through to me,
and I need to get through to them—
to get through high positions and status and high walls.
I want to be an equal,
among all the different kinds.
Lord, I don't want to be ashamed of my age,
of being too old or too young,
and I don't want others to use their age against me.
Take away the big competition.
Make us a community, Jesus.

I Want to Be an Equal

Lord, I pray for the old.
Lord, there are all the old people in the world.
They have been places I'll never go.
They have lived in times which will never return.
Help me do more
than read where they have lived.
Help me to talk to the old
and hear them tell of the past.
I need to know who are old.
Give me the ability to be open to them,
to ask them questions, and to enjoy them.
In being young, may I not overlook those
who have succeeded in growing old.
Give me the sense
to feel their feelings, Jesus.

I Pray for the Old

Lord, I need the prayers of others.
Something happens to me when people care,
when others pray for me.
Lord, there are prayers being said for me
in all the world.
People petition in my behalf.
I am remembered.
I am prayed for and you hear these prayers.
I need to remember that I am remembered
in your large family.
They love me.
They pray for what I need.
They thank for what I have.
They ask for what I do.
They care for me. You know it, Jesus.
Remind me, so I know it too, Jesus.

They Care for Me

Lord, what do I do with all the speeches.
Lord, some of the speeches get so long.
The words pile up and I feel covered by them.
The sentences get in the way of each other.
They cancel each other out.
I need some space for all the words that keep coming to me.
Give me some places and people
who will let me sit and be silent,
and not say anything.
I need such a place,
for all the words to be quiet and for me to hear their meaning.
Thank you
that the world does not run out of prayer places,
and quiet spaces,
and people who let me come and be, Jesus.

I Need Such a Place

Lord, we are not all looking at things in the same way.
We see the same thing happening,
and we're not agreed on what we see and feel.
We are many,
and together we make up a world of differences.
Help us to take the time
to know what one another knows and feels,
so that we can increase what is true.
We cannot see so much alone;
we cannot decide all the truth alone.
We do not need to do it alone;
we have one another.
Improve our sight
as we look and feel and talk and act with others.
We have each other, Jesus.
How much we learn when we look again, Jesus.

We Have One Another

Increase My Feelings

Lord, ideas keep coming into my head,
and I don't know where they come from.
They seem to come from deep inside myself,
and they also come from the outside.
In me there lives so much that is new and original,
I'm glad for the gift of new thoughts.
Remind this day of the importance of the human mind.
I am responsible;
I am imaginative.
Come to me in my mind, Jesus.

Come to Me in My Mind

Lord, I like to live.
I have a lot of feeling for things and people.
There's a lot going on I don't seem to see.
I need to know where the real life is,
where the joy is,
where the need is,
where the peace is.
I want to get all I can out of life;
and I want to give it back.
Keep me curious in all my senses.
Don't let me quit having a lot of feeling for what's going on,
here and anywhere.
Make me more aware as I get older.
Increase my feelings.
Bring me to my senses, Jesus.

Increase My Feelings

Lord, I have an adventurous spirit.
There used to be land and islands to discover.
They have been found . . . and people live on them.
I know that pioneering is a chapter in history books.
I know that paintings of pioneers hang in museums.
But, Lord, I want to be a pioneer too.
I want to discover. I love the new.
Let me pioneer polluted land and water.
Lord, I want to rediscover it.
I want to reclaim
what is lost in erosion and waste.
Make me a pioneer,
and send me to discover and reclaim
what is ahead.
I'll go west, or south, or I'll do it right here.
Not everything has been found,
so send me, Jesus.

I Want to Be a Pioneer

Lord, I'm feeling good.
I feel like a million dollars.
I feel like a new house with a family moving in.
I feel like a trout going upstream in June.
I feel like a bird making a spring nest.
I feel good as a garden in a soft rain.
Like a sidewalk patched carefully.
Like a team that has just won its first game,
when everybody said they couldn't.
I feel good, Lord.
I feel forgiven. I belong.
Keep me thinking about how good it feels
to feel good, Jesus.

How Good It Feels

Lord, I need to laugh.
Why did you make us able to laugh?
What is the good of laughing?
What if I could not laugh again?
Lord, how can I use laughing in these times?
What is laughing to the gospel?
Lord, how could I live without it?
I laugh at what surprises me and makes me glad.
I laugh when something is strange,
and when I'm surprised.
I laugh when I'm surrounded by people who love me.
I laugh when I'm not able to cry.
I laugh when something is ridiculous.
Lord, bless my sense of humor.
Increase my surprises
and the times I am caught by surprise.
Even the thought of the resurrection
can make me laugh.
It is such good news,
and such a surprise, Jesus.

Bless My Sense of Humor

Lord, I like the dark.
Lord, there is freedom in the dark.
I can shut my eyes, and I can remember
what I thought I had forgotten.
I can see what happened long ago.
I can shut my eyes and dream.
In the dark I can hear more.
In the dark I can hear the moving traffic
like streaks of curved sounds.
Lord, there is something very good about the dark.
You made the night and gave it to me.
May I not forget the dark,
and fill it with fear.
May I not sleep it all away,
or miss it in the glare of electric lights.
Make the dark more holy to me.
Come in the meditation and the moods of night
and enlighten me in your dark.
How much good there is in the dark, Jesus.

Make the Dark More Holy

Lord, give me the daring spirit of a clown
on a trapeze.
Give my mind the freedom to jump
on a high wire.
I need the courage and the skill
to take chances in public.
Give me nerve.
Help me to focus all my abilities and skills
so I can risk and have courage.
Let me think a good thing and do it
and keep my balance in everything.
Bring me peace.
Bring together all that is in my mind and spirit,
and the talents of my body, so I can have peace.
I have this peace from you.
Lord, make me go where nobody is going.
Make me your daring clown, Jesus.

Give Me Nerve

Lord, send me somewhere new.
Give me a feeling only I can have
and a view only I can see,
a sound only I can hear,
an emotion only I can feel,
an idea only I can think,
and a hope only I can have.
Make me me.
Give me a new look at myself
so that in this new way
I can see what I have
and who I am.
Help me to sort out
and put together
in some quick way,
and to know what I need to know.
Separate me from things
that blur my perception.
Give me a glimpse of myself.
Send me to do something
that is for me to do.
Show me myself.
May I accept myself
as much as you accept me,
and as gladly, Jesus.

Make Me Me

Lord, there are times
when I do not celebrate.
Life is a bore,
the world passes by,
and talking seems useless.
Days come,
and nights go,
and things don't seem to change
or make a difference.
Yesterday and today are the same.
I am out of touch.
When will you
break into my prison
and start a celebration?
Do it to me.
Then send me to someone,
also silent and imprisoned,
to start your celebration there, Jesus.

I Am Out of Touch

Lord, you know my beginning.
Before I could say my very first word,
I cried and laughed
and felt and touched and received
and I gave.
I could only be, without saying anything about it.
Everything I did
I did with my hands, my feet,
my mouth, my eyes, my body;
my body was my entire vocabulary.
Then came my first word,
and the next, Lord.
And then came the sentences,
and now the paragraphs
and all the pages.
I know volumes of words.
O Lord, sometimes take me to my beginning—
to do and to be,
to be myself,
to cry, to laugh, to feel, to touch,
to receive and to give.
Bring me to all my senses, Jesus.

Take Me to My Beginning

Lord, I need to find
a secret place
where I have never been.
I need it for a thought I do not know,
and for an emotion that is new to me.
Lord, I need a coming together of things.
I need for some old things to be like new
and for some new things to be old.
My mind needs to be opened,
my feelings turned on,
and my senses sharpened.
I want to feel what had no feeling for me,
and to see where I saw nothing.
I want to hear where I was like deaf
and to understand
what was boring before.
I want to be like new.
Send another miracle to me.
Alleluia to you,
and glory, and praise, and power,
and thanks to you, Jesus.

I Want to Be Like New

Keep Coming Jesus

Lord, how could the people wait so long
for your birth?
How could they hope
and not give up?
How does a nation wait
for a thousand years?
Thanks for the patience and the hope
that keeps each day open.
I like to expect.
I like to get ready.
I like to know a celebration is coming.
You are not old and out of date.
You are new and for the future.
For the next generation.
For the next century.
For next year.
For tomorrow.
Lord, you put us in this life
in which things keep happening,
and you keep coming.
So take us on.
Keep coming, and keep us going, Jesus.

I Like to Get Ready

Lord, Christmas is on my mind.
I am amazed at the miracle
of you so visible on earth,
of you once less than 21 inches long
and crying in a manger.
But who can comprehend
all that was on your mind
as you entered the earth in this way?
Math and science help me to comprehend
your creative mind.
Social needs can help me comprehend
the love in your redemptive mind.
When I see how we live
and how we need love,
then I know why your birth happened.
Keep coming
when we least expect you
and where we most need you, Jesus.

Keep Coming, Jesus

Lord, they couldn't keep the story of your birth
to themselves.
It barely began,
and kings were carrying it east
and shepherds to the hills.
Lord, what are the ways to tell the story today?
It seems they all have heard it.
We've all seen the story
in some commercial form.
What can I say
that goes deeper into the story?
How can I get past the pageantry?
How can I get to what it's really about?
Tell me and show me
the story of your salvation once more,
so I can hear it like new
and see it as though for the first time.
Keep me from being bored.
Keep me from being scared.
Keep me wide awake
in this world.
When salvation happens,
let me see it.
Then make me run with it, Jesus.

Show Me the Story

Lord, I know you really meant it.
You didn't fool around in the holy city.
You didn't pretend and hide, Jesus.
You walked straight into the problems,
and you never faked it.
You broke open the rules
that had lost their meaning.
You brought life back
to the dead law of the land.
You put spirit back into the cruel crowds
and courage into hearts.
You gave a day meaning.
That's what I want:
meaning, purpose,
a reason to do it, to say it, to feel it, to make it,
a reason for getting up and for facing it,
a reason to change it.
You knew that it was always all about meaning.
It still is, Lord;
it has to mean something.
You looked for it and found it.
So will I, Jesus.

I Want Meaning

Lord, send me a surprise.
One that catches me off guard
and makes me wonder.
Like Easter.
Send me a resurrection
when everything looks dead and buried.
Send me light
when the night seems too long.
Send me spring
when the cold and frozen season seems endless.
Send me a new idea
when my mind is empty.
Send me a thing to do
when I am just waiting around.
Send me a new friend
when I am alone.
Send me peace
when I'm afraid.
Send me a future
when it looks hopeless.
Send me your resurrection
when I die, Jesus.

Send Me a Surprise

Lord, your Holy Spirit did come,
and there is great power on earth.
There is enormous power
within us and between us.
Open up my potential.
Open up my eyes to see
what goes by unseen.
Open my ears to hear
what I never hear.
Open my mind to think
what I have never given a thought to.
Open my emotions to feel
what I have not dared to feel.
Open my spirit to believe
what I go around doubting.
Put the power to work
and multiply the strength of my life.
Inspire me to do more.
As I grow in days,
may I increase in power and in your Spirit, Jesus.

Put the Power to Work

Lord, you will come again.
You will come with power,
and it will be mine.
You will come with glory
and show it to me.
You will wipe away tears,
and I will give up sadness.
You will wipe out death,
and I will live forever.
You will come,
and I will see you as you are.
You will say, "It is I,"
and I will know you said it.
You will return,
and I will live on,
when you come again come in power and glory, Jesus.

You Will Return